The River Trent

on old postcards

Brian Lund

1. The river bank near Trent Bridge, West Bridgford, was always incredibly popular with the local population seeking a relaxing afternoon out. This view is on a postcard published by local firm C. & A.G. Lewis about 1923.

ISBN 0 946245 67 3

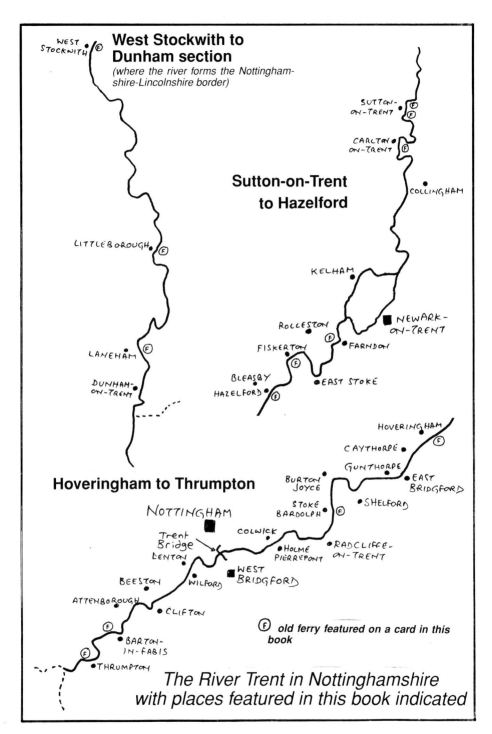

West Stockwith to Dunham section
(where the river forms the Nottinghamshire-Lincolnshire border)

Sutton-on-Trent to Hazelford

Hoveringham to Thrumpton

Ⓕ **old ferry featured on a card in this book**

The River Trent in Nottinghamshire with places featured in this book indicated

Designed and published by
Reflections of a Bygone Age,
Keyworth, Nottingham 1993
Reprinted 1996 and 2001

THE TRENT IN FLOOD, NOTTINGHAM

2. The river flooded regularly before the Great War, as shown on a 'Peveril' series card posted from Nottingham in October 1911. One of the advertising hoardings on the right is for the "Hippodrome".

Printed by
Adlard Print and Typesetting Services,
Ruddington, Notts.

Acknowledgements: thanks to the following for the loan of cards used in this book: Peter Cooke (8, 15), Pete Davies (1, 12, 17), Tim Farr (2, 5, 11, 19-20, 24, 28, 33-37, 39-40, 42-43, 48-50, 52, 54-57), Graham Hopcroft (7), Grenville Jennings (3), David Ottewell (44-45).

INTRODUCTION

At the end of the twentieth century, with road transport dominating the carriage of goods and people throughout Nottinghamshire – even the role of the railways has been severely diminished in the last three decades – it is sometimes difficult to imagine how important the River Trent once was to the county's economy and growth. Towns and villages grew up around the river, and facilities for transportation and warehousing sprang up along its navigable length.

This book features the River Trent within Nottinghamshire as portrayed by old picture postcards, mostly those published in the period between 1902 and 1939. That first date marked the start of a craze in Britain for sending and collecting picture postcards, which served in Edwardian times much as the telephone does today. The years up to 1914 were the 'Golden Age' of postcards, when millions of imaginative designs covering every subject under the sun were published by a host of national and local firms.

Even by Edwardian times, the important role played by the Trent had diminished as railways had taken much of its trade, but the postcards illustrated here clearly show the activities still centred on the river. Ferry crossings existed then at many points, and riverside pubs were commonplace. The ferries have now gone, and new road bridges have been built at key locations.

A wide selection of publishers of postcards is featured in this book, including some who seemed to prefer to remain anonymous. One of the most prolific local series was the 'Clumber', published by Albert Hindley (who ran a stationery shop on Clumber Street in Nottingham) in the 1905-8 period. After the First World War, C. & A.G. Lewis of Nottingham included many river scenes in their comprehensive coverage of the county. Some fine hotel advertising cards by Howard Barrett of Southwell are included, too. National firms like W.H. Smith, Francis Frith of Reigate, and Valentine of Dundee featured those areas judged to have a high postcard sales potential.

Through the medium of these cards, we can see the River Trent in a more leisurely age, when a crossing more than likely meant a trip on a ferry boat and picnics by the riverside were enlivened by barges on the water. In many ways, though, the Trent is still an idyll for fishermen and leisure pursuits, and its banks still populated by grazing cows.

Brian Lund
July 1993

Front cover: Royal academy exhibitor Charles Edwin Flower captured the romance of Trent Bridge on a postcard published in 1904 by Raphael Tuck of London. Punting, rowing and relaxing are all part of a timeless summer scene. The "Town Arms" public house has been renamed the "Aviary" within the last decade, and the bridge itself was improved in the 1920s. On the right, beyond the bridge, is part of an exhibition/entertainment complex *(see illus. 65).* Card in Tuck's 'Oilette' series, no. 1783, one of six views by Flower featuring Nottingham scenes.

Back cover (top): a postcard in the 'City & Wollaton' series, posted from Nottingham to Newport Pagnell in August 1911.

(bottom): one of a set of six comic photographic postcards published by C. & A.G. Lewis, with artist F.H. Martin's drawings superimposed onto a river scene. This example was posted to Coventry in May 1919.

3. Thrumpton's ferry crossing, one of many along the River Trent in Nottinghamshire which are featured in this book. 'Clumber' series postcard, posted at Long Eaton in April 1906.

4. The site of the old ferry crossing at Barton-in-Fabis, where the river is half-a-mile from the village. 'Peveril' real photo series card from c. 1920.

5. Barton ferry with a full complement of passengers. 'Clumber' series postcard, published about 1906.

6. The weir at Beeston, with the lock which marks the western end of the Beeston canal in the distance on the right. A sunny afternoon in 1905 has attracted a large number of children as well as a group of adults in the foreground. The writer, who lived at Humber Grove in Beeston, reckoned this was a *"favourite spot"*.

RIVER TRENT, BEESTON.

7. A busy summer scene on the River Trent as a pleasure steamer appears narrowly to miss a rowing boat with two ladies aboard. Families on the far bank queue for a trip on the steamer. No. 100 in C. and A.G. Lewis's series.

Peveril Series.   KIRKE WHITE'S COTTAGE, NOTTINGHAM.

8. Nottingham poet Henry Kirke White (1785-1806) lived in this cottage by the Trent near Clifton. 'Peveril' series card.

120   CLIFTON HALL, FROM BEESTON.

9. Clifton Hall, part of the Trent University campus, was originally built for Gervase Clifton.

GROVE FARM, TRENT SIDE, LENTON, NOTTM.

10. Grove Farm, near the Clifton road bridge, features on an Edwardian postcard. The area near the farm now houses a range of sports fields.

AERIAL PICTURE : H.R.H. THE PRINCE OF WALES' FARM—IN FLOOD—MAY 24TH, 1932.
Photo : " The Scribe " " Nottingham Evening News.

11. Floods in 1932 provide a spectacular picture of the Prince of Wales' farm at Lenton. The aerial view postcard was published by a local newspaper.

WILFORD BRIDGE. NOTTINGHAM

12. The old toll bridge at Wilford, built in 1870 by E.W. Hughes. The tollgate and house are to the right, off picture. The statue in the foreground is of Sir Robert Jukes Clifton. 'Clumber' series card no.122.

13. St. Wilfrid's Church at Wilford features on the left of this postcard, published by Valentine and posted to Coventry in December 1914. *"Having a jolly time after a tedious railway journey. Have not seen any Germans yet but seen plenty of lace making"*, wrote May. The 14th century church has memorial windows to Kirke White *(see illus. 8)* who lived in Wilford for many years.

14. The magnificent (for a footbridge) suspension bridge which connects Victoria Embankment with West Bridgford was built in 1906 and is seen here shortly after it was opened. The card was sent from a resident of West Avenue in Bridgford on 4th October 1907 to Long Eaton.

15. A card published by C. and A.G. Lewis in the 1920s, with plenty of people enjoying the river embankment. The building on the south side is the masonic hall.

TRENT BRIDGE, NOTTS. DURING DROUGHT   PEVERIL SERIES

16. Hundreds of people crowd onto Trent Bridge to watch the spectacle of a declining river during a summer drought. The year is unclear, but the 'Peveril' series card seems to be of c.1913 vintage. Trent Bridge was built in 1871 to replace a 10th century structure, and was widened to cope with more traffic in 1924-6.

-11-

17. Nottingham has hosted rowing clubs on the river for many years. This W.H. Smith 'Kingsway' series card was posted in May 1908 and shows part of the complex built for the Midlands Exhibition of 1903 *(see illus. 65)*.

18. A fine panoramic view looking towards Trent Bridge, showing the new landscaping programme paid for by Jesse Boot in 1920. The postcard, published by Spree, gives the precise date of the photograph: 14th July 1921. This example was posted to Skegness in September 1922.

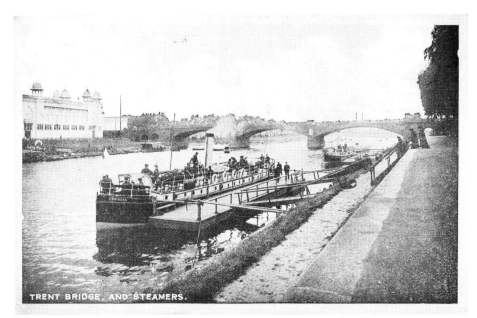

19. The steamer *Empress,* one of the pleasure boats that plied the river. 'Jaysee' series card, posted at Mansfield in May 1916.

20. Holbein, a famous channel swimmer from Nottingham, beginning a river exhibition swim at Trent Bridge in 1905. The 'Peveril' series card was posted at Nottingham in May of that year.

LANDING STAGE, COLWICK PARK, NOTTINGHAM.

21. Pleasure trips from Trent Bridge terminated at Colwick Park. No shortage of customers on this W.H. Smith card, posted in January 1914 at Stapleford.

COLWICK WEIR, NOTTINGHAM

22. Colwick Weir, near Holme Lock, on another postcard published by W.H. Smith, and posted at Nottingham in September 1917.

23. Colwick Vale housing was always susceptible to flooding, as can be seen from this card featuring a scene in December 1910.

24. A barge belonging to the Trent Navigation Co. is seen moored near Holme Pierrepont lock on a 'Clumber' series card.

25. The wharf at Radcliffe-on-Trent on 'Peveril' series card no.551, which was actually posted at Manchester in April 1921. A caravan park is now adjacent to this scene at a point where the river bends sharply.

River Trent, Radcliffe.

Taylor.   *Radcliffe.*

26. Peaceful contentment at Radcliffe at the turn of the century. Cows grazing on the southern bank of the river are still a feature from here to Fiskerton. Card by H. Taylor of Radcliffe, posted to Blackpool in June 1904.

The River Trent at Radcliffe.

27. The *Little John* steam barge towing a sailing barge on the river at Radcliffe.

The Ferry, Stoke Bardolph.

28. The old ferry at Stoke Bardolph used a rope pulley. The ferry is featured on a post-card by C. & A.G. Lewis, looking towards the south (Shelford) bank where the boat is moored. Today the slipway on the Stoke side is still there, near the "Ferry Boat" Inn *(see also back cover).*

29. The *Little John* makes another appearance, this time near Burton Joyce (the village church is in the background).

PEVERIL REAL PHOTO SERIES   UNICORN HOTEL. GUNTHORPE. NOTTS.

30. Many hotels were built on the banks of the Trent to cater for both river and road traffic. The "Unicorn", still flourishing today at Gunthorpe, features on a 'Peveril' series card, posted at Gedling in July 1928. The photograph was taken from the East Bridgford side of the river.

31. The original road bridge at Gunthorpe on an un-numbered 'Clumber' series post-card.

32. A new bridge here was essential to cater for the increasing volume of traffic that wanted to use it. Gunthorpe's new crossing was opened ceremoniously by the Prince of Wales (later Edward VIII) in 1924. The scene was captured on a photographic card by Spree.

33. This view in the 'Clumber' series can also be found with the caption *'East Bridgford, Notts'*. This village is just a few hundred yards from the south bank of the river.

34. At Caythorpe the Dover Beck, which flows south from Oxton, enters the Trent. C. & A.G. Lewis card no. 903.

35. Trent Navigation Co. barge at Hoveringham on a postcard by J.H. Scott of Bulcote.

36. The ferry at Hoveringham pictured on a 'Clumber' series card posted at Derby in October 1905. The sender wrote: *"am going to the Empire tonight"*. The white building on the right was the boathouse, demolished in the late 1960s.

37. Lovely advertising card for the "Old Elm Tree" Hotel at Hoveringham, whose proprietor, when this was published by Howard Barrett of Southwell, was James Sadler. The ferry is seen in the foreground. The hotel has been converted into private housing, part of which bears the original name.

James Sadler, Proprietor.

Wines, Spirits & Cigars of the Best Quality,

...erside Resort,

38. The "Star and Garter" Hotel at Hazleford (sic) Ferry near the village of Bleasby. Another Barrett card, published about 1916. Note the grazing cows.

39. C. & A.G. Lewis postcard of the same hotel in the early 1920s. Today it is known as the "Hazelford Ferry".

40. The ferry at Fiskerton seen on a card posted in August 1914. The site of the battle of East Stoke is just opposite here.

41. Fishing wear has changed dramatically since J. Henry Scott of Bulcote published this card of a fishing match at Rolleston just before the Great War. At this point of the river, though, the closest village is actually Farndon on the south bank.

" BROMLEY ARMS," FISKERTON, NOTTS.

Photographed & Published by Howard Barrett, Southwell.
Patronised by His Majesty the King.

The place to

42. Fiskerton is unusual in that part of the village lies along the banks of the river. The "Bromley Arms" appears on a similar advertising card to illus. 37. The pub is still there, but the bridge in the picture has been pulled down and replaced by a concrete wall. Fiskerton Wharf is to the left of this scene.

G. PACEY   Proprietor.

Wines, Spirits, and Cigars of the best quality.

1 a happy day.

Farndon Ferry.

43. Farndon Ferry viewed from the Rolleston side on a photographic card posted in October 1914: *"The fishing is dead off, and also is the weather. We had to walk from Newark on Saturday as the man failed to turn up as things are getting very dear. I would advise getting something in."* The Great War was just two months old.

44. Newark owed much of its importance and growth to its position on the River Trent, and there was a crossing point here from the 12th century. On this card by Frith of Reigate are Parnham's watermill (left), a dredger, and the chimneys of the Trent Brewery in Millgate.

45. Another Frith postcard featuring the castle and footbridge, and, in the distance, the road bridge. The castle was begun in 1125, became a royalist stronghold in the Civil War, and was then partially demolished on the orders of Parliament in the 1650s.

46. Boating on the river at Newark. Valentine's published this card in the 1920s.

2987. The Old Lock House, N

47. The old Nether Lock between Newark and Winthorpe. In the mist in the background is the Midland Railway bridge. The paddle steamer could be one owned by Watsons of Gainsborough. When this postcard was published by Spree in the 1920's, this was the only lock between Newark and the sea.

48. The bridge at Kelham, a five-arch red brick construction built in 1957. Past Farndon, the Trent divides into two, one winding past Kelham Hall, the other under the walls of Newark Castle, before re-uniting at Winthorpe.

THE TRENT, COLLINGHAM.

49. Fishing on the Trent at Collingham on an Edwardian-period postcard by unidentified publisher.

50. The ferry at Carlton-on-Trent, near the wharf which at one time catered for heavy traffic on the river. The remains of an old tower mill are on the right.

51. Meering ferry at Sutton-on-Trent on a 'Peveril' series card.

52. Sutton's other ferry, Marnham, is included on this multi-view card published by Frith of Reigate, along with Meering and three local country houses.

53. The river at Sutton-on-Trent on an anonymously-published postcard of about 1910.

54. Dunham Bridge over the Trent near Tuxford. Card published by Wrench of London and posted from Sutton-on-Trent in December 1907.

55. Two views of the Trent on this multi-view postcard of Laneham, including one showing Moore's mill. *"This postcard shows parts of our village, and the mill where I lived for 9 years after leaving home,"* wrote the sender of this card posted at the village in August 1917.

56. The Romans used this crossing of the Trent at Littleborough as a ford. It's seen here on a card published by Edgar Welchman of Retford.

57. West Stockwith ferry, the most northerly point of the Trent in Nottinghamshire. A horse and cart is being transported on a barge across the river.

(please note: cards on inside back cover numbered in error and should read 58 and 59).